GLORY U

The icon depicting the transfiguration of Jesus, shown on the front cover, was painted by Brother Anselm, OSB of Alton Abbey.

Glory Under Your Feet

From Transfiguration to Transformation

Six Bible studies on the transfiguration of
the Church and the transformation of society

BISHOP MICHAEL MARSHALL

Marshall Pickering
An Imprint of HarperCollins*Publishers*

Marshall Pickering is an Imprint of
HarperCollins*Religious*
Part of HarperCollins*Publishers*
77–85 Fulham Palace Road, London W6 8JB

First published in Great Britain
in 1996 by Marshall Pickering

1 3 5 7 9 10 8 6 4 2

A catalogue record for this book is
available from the British Library

0551 030461

Printed and bound in Great Britain by
Woolnough Bookbinding Limited,
Irthlingborough, Northamptonshire

Acknowledgements

The author is deeply grateful to the following people for the support, prayerful encouragement and practical help which they gave him while he was writing this small manual for pilgrims: Charles Longbottom and Russ Parker of the Acorn Christian Healing Trust; Michael Mitton of Anglican Renewal Ministries; and John Richardson, the Provost of Bradford. These four met with and prayed with the author for nearly two years, and out of that fellowship the vision for a National Cathedrals' Prayer Pilgrimage – called 'Glory Under Your Feet' – was conceived. The pilgrimage took place in the summer of 1996.

In the course of writing this book at break-neck speed the author received many helpful suggestions from his colleagues and fellow pilgrims. *Deo Gratias.*

The whole team who undertook the Cathedrals' Pilgrimage are especially grateful to Brother Anselm,

OSB of Alton Abbey, for painting the icon of the Transfiguration which was carried round from cathedral to cathedral in the course of the pilgrimage and is gloriously portrayed on the cover of this book.

Contents

The Transfiguration of Jesus Christ According to St Luke

Now about eight days after these sayings he [Jesus] took with him Peter and John and James, and went up on the mountain to pray. And as he was praying, the appearance of his countenance was altered, and his raiment became dazzling white. And behold, two men talked with him, Moses and Elijah, who appeared in glory and spoke of his departure, which he was to accomplish at Jerusalem. Now Peter and those who were with him were heavy with sleep but kept awake, and they saw his glory and the two men who stood with him. And as the men were parting from him, Peter said to Jesus, 'Master, it is well that we are here; let us make three booths, one for you and one for Moses and one for Elijah' – not knowing what he said. As he said this, a cloud came and overshadowed them; and they were afraid as they entered the cloud. And a voice came out of the cloud, saying, 'This is my Son, my Chosen; listen to him!' And when the voice had spoken, Jesus was found alone. And they kept silence and told no one in those days anything of what they had seen.

On the next day, when they had come down from the mountain, a great crowd met him.

(LUKE 9:28–37, RSV)

The End in the Middle

'But,' [the LORD] said, 'you cannot see my face; for man shall not see me and live.' And the LORD said, 'Behold, there is a place by me where you shall stand upon the rock; and while my glory passes by I will put you in a cleft of the rock, and I will cover you with my hand until I have passed by; then I will take away my hand, and you shall see my back; but my face shall not be seen.'

(EXODUS 33:20–23)

Change and Purpose

'So what on earth is the point of it all?' we frequently ask ourselves. Faced with the trauma of change and the decision-making of daily life, we are sorely tempted simply to opt out, or to spin a coin, or to read our horoscope. For if I cannot see the end result – the point of it all – then, when I am faced with the need to make choices (moral or otherwise) at the crossroads, or just at a fork in the road, there is no such thing as a right or a wrong turning. If we do not know where we are going, there is no such thing as a right or wrong way to get there. Often, it is only when we arrive at our destination that we can tell whether or not we have made the right choice.

Change

'To live is to change,' wrote Cardinal Newman, 'and to be perfect is to have changed often.' Today things are changing on every front, more rapidly than in any previous age. There is a strong possibility that many of these changes are not only damaging but also irreversible. Economically, environmentally, socially and genetically, all kinds of changes are taking place in our own day. So often these changes appear to be determined by 'them' – by faceless and anonymous forces over which we have little or no control. Many of the fears which are current in our society originate from this sense that change is out of control and drifting aimlessly, without direction, purpose or goal. Little wonder, as we near the end of the millennium, that there is much fear abroad about the shape of things to come.

The End Product and Purpose of It All

'You'll never catch me going up in one of those things', the caterpillar is reported to have said to a passing butterfly! From a caterpillar's point of view, the prospect of radical changes in one's life-style means the challenge of leaping into the unknown. 'Yet just suppose,' we might want to say to that grounded caterpillar, 'just suppose that two-dimensional caterpillars were created precisely in order to become three-dimensional butterflies. Then surely the vision of a passing butterfly, far from constituting a threat, represents an exciting invitation!' Similarly with human beings. Just suppose that three-dimensional human beings were intended to become multi-dimensional creatures and to live for ever. Then surely that's quite another story altogether and puts quite a different perspective on the whole discussion about change and direction.

'I have come,' said Jesus, 'in order that you might have life and have it in all its fullness' (John

10:10). Jesus came to show us the intended end-product of the human race – what we are intended to look like at the end of the day. Jesus Christ shows us God's way of being truly and fully human – what life is really all about. He shows us not only where we have come from, but – perhaps much more importantly – also where we are going, the point and purpose of it all. We can all empathize with the character in Lennon and McCartney's famous song, 'Nowhere Man', who feels he is going nowhere and living a pointless existence. For life without purpose is little better than death.

What End Do We Have in View?

As we approach the third millennium, many people are beginning to ask what sort of society under God we should be attempting to create for our children. Where are the changes which we are now making likely to lead, further down the road of history? Are they changes for the better, and if so, then against what are they to be measured? What are the forces at work in our society which make for a better quality of life – a life which is truly human rather than the programmed existence of a robot?

The Mind and Purpose of the Maker

Faced with any product, it is surely never a bad idea to consult the manufacturer's user-friendly guide. Christians believe that in the Bible and in the person of Jesus Christ, to whom the Bible points, we have such a guide. The Bible shows us the purpose for which we were created, and in Christ we catch a glimpse of the 'finished product' – of the kind of people God intended human beings to be.

'The glory of God is a human being fully alive,' wrote Irenaeus at the end of the second century, while 'the life of humanity consists in the vision of God.' Made in God's image, we need to recapture a glimpse of the glory of God and of what it is that makes God God, if we are to know what will make us who we were truly made to be. Christians believe that Jesus Christ came into history as 'the end in the middle' – to show us the point of it all; to show us where suffering and the human struggle are intended to lead, so that neither daily life in particular nor human history in general may degenerate into just 'one darned thing after another'!

The Transfiguration of Christ – Larger than Life

It is not accidental that the accounts of the transfiguration of Jesus are central to the three gospels of Matthew, Mark and Luke. They constitute the turning point in our understanding of the gospel message of Jesus. The transfiguration event takes us right to the heart of the matter. As Jesus takes up his journey and sets his face towards Jerusalem (Luke 9:51), Calvary and ultimately the heavenly Jerusalem, that road takes him and all who follow him right through the injustice, the darkness and the pain of the world. On that mountain top, Jesus gives to the inner cabinet of his friends – Peter, James and John – a glimpse of the end in the middle, so to speak – the point of it all, right in the midst of it all.

As Jesus the God-man shows us his glory on the sacred mountain, so, through the eyes of those three disciples, he shows us what all men and women are intended to become. He shows us humanity in all its richness, glory and beauty; people as they were originally created to be. He shows us a quality of life which is larger than life!

On the Way and All the Way

The painful struggle to recover that first beauty and image is beyond our unaided grasp – though artists, philosophers and musicians have instinctively tried to reach out for it. However, Christians believe that, at last, God has plunged himself into the whole torrent of the evolutionary struggle in the person of Jesus of Nazareth, and in so doing he has marked out a path and a pilgrimage which leads to a new quality of life. This path fully takes into account the pain and the struggle of life, ending and coming to completion in purpose and glory.

It's one thing to put a man on the moon, but quite another to restore humanity back to where we ultimately belong – in the heart of God for ever. Such a vision will give point and purpose to history. Without such 'a vision, the people perish' (Proverbs 29:18). Our journey to that mountain of transfiguration, in heart and mind, is a pilgrimage with Jesus Christ as our Guide in the vanguard, encouraging us to grow as we travel, and to change from glory to glory as we advance along the road of human history.

This little book of meditations and reflections on the transfiguration was originally written for the National Cathedrals' Prayer Mission which took place in the summer of 1996. However, it has a more general use for all pilgrims and disciples who are followers in the way, and it is intended to encourage all seekers, by pointing us to Jesus, 'the pioneer and perfecter' of this whole process of discipleship (see Hebrews 12:2). At each step of our pilgrimage we shall be challenged with a three-point agenda: *renewal*, *healing* and *evangelism*.

Healing, Renewal and Evangelism

At various points on the way, we shall need to seek healing, help and counselling for our souls as well as for our bodies. Yet renewal, refreshment and regeneration await us at every turning of the road if we will avail ourselves of the services of the hospices and the hospitality of the many well-located roadside taverns – the sacraments of the Church, the guidance of the Scriptures and the abiding presence of God's own Spirit to accompany us as we travel. They will lead us, as Scripture promises, into the fullness of life and truth – namely, Jesus Christ, who is himself the Way, the Truth and the Life.

Like all pilgrims throughout the ages, as we travel we shall share our stories, sing our songs and help to care for each other's wounds, and in so doing we shall recover our true identity. Furthermore, it will not be long before we realize that we are part of a larger company of men and women on the move, with glory under our feet, with purpose and destination on the horizon, following our leader, 'who for the joy that was set before him, endured the cross, despising the shame, and is seated at the right hand of the throne of God' (Hebrews 12:2), preparing a place for us.

Using This Book

Pilgrimage and Travelling

This book is a prayerful study of the accounts of the transfiguration of Jesus in the gospels of Matthew, Mark and Luke. The best way to use it would be in the context of pilgrimage – perhaps by travelling to a holy place such as a shrine or a cathedral, or by going to a special part of your home which is set aside for quiet and reflection – and so to use the physical journey (however short or long) as a kind of 'sacrament' of an inner journey of reflection, exploration and study.

Study and Reflection

This book is intended to help 'pilgrims of the heart' to move from one perspective to another in ways similar to those experienced on a physical journey. It should help us to see not so much a different world, but rather the same old world from a very different point of view.

Corporate and Personal

This book can be used individually for personal reflection or in a group. It was originally designed to be used in the context of a pilgrimage. However, it can equally well be used over a period of six weeks, with a Bible-study group meeting every week to pray over, discuss and reflect upon the questions which arise from it.

The point of this whole exercise is to bring about a change of heart, a change of outlook and a new perspective – in other words, a transfiguration and therefore a transformation. For ultimately, only a transfigured Church can call for a transformation of society.

CHAPTER 1

From Looking to Worshipping

Now about eight days after these sayings he [Jesus] took with him Peter and John and James, and went up on the mountain to pray. And as he was praying, the appearance of his countenance was altered, and his raiment became dazzling white. And behold, two men talked with him, Moses and Elijah, who appeared in glory and spoke of his departure, which he was to accomplish at Jerusalem. Now Peter and those who were with him were heavy with sleep but kept awake, and they saw his glory and the two men who stood with him.

(LUKE 9:28–32)

Christian discipleship is an invitation to journey and to travel with Christ as our fellow Pilgrim and Guide. Christians were not originally called Christians, but simply 'followers in the Way' (Acts 11:26).

Augustine wrote, 'Thither we make our way, still as pilgrims, not yet at rest; still on the road, not yet home; still aiming at it, not yet attaining it.'[1] At a special turning point on that return journey homewards to heaven – a journey which passes right through the heart of the pain and darkness of the world – Jesus gave to that inner circle of his closest friends a remarkable encounter in which he showed them the point of it all – the glory of God. On that mountain 'they saw his glory', we are told. They 'were eye-witnesses of his majesty' (2 Peter 1:16). Some eye-opener!

On that mountain top, Jesus invited the three disciples to look, to listen, to learn – not just with their physical eyes and ears but also with what St Augustine calls 'the eyes and ears of the heart'. Only if we are fully awake, with eyes and ears wide open, will we be able to see the glory of God – as the gospel accounts tell us the three disciples did. 'Wake up!' is the clarion call of the gospel. Sadly, most of us, most of the time, are only half awake and indeed half alive!

Jesus invited those three disciples to see the whole of life from a new perspective – from a different point of view. From that mountain top they could see the road in the valley below, leading up to

Jerusalem and to the pain and suffering of the crucifixion, of which Jesus had spoken only eight days earlier.

That was the road which Jesus himself was about to walk. He invited all his disciples to follow in the same way, which leads to real life *beyond* – to the glory of God and to the life of wonder and worship. Worship is not a matter of seeing a different world – that would be escapism. Rather, worship is seeing the same old world very differently. 'Good God, now I see!' we exclaim. Of course, it was staring us in the face all along, but we couldn't see the wood for the trees.

'As Jesus was praying, the appearance of his countenance was altered.' A praying church will look very different from a church that is not praying. As we look at life from a different point of view, we ourselves begin to look different. When we fall in love we begin to look different because we are seeing life from a totally new perspective. As one of Andrew Lloyd Webber's songs says, 'Love changes everything.' Looking differently leads to looking different! We could equally well say, 'Worship changes everything.'

For worship is not a mere therapy to give us the 'feel-good factor'. It demands that we change our whole outlook on the whole of life. Worship which does not issue in discipleship is dangerous and potentially evil. In true worship voyeurs are turned into voyagers! As Ann and Barry Ulanov have written, real prayer is 'taking the risk of exposing ourselves to an ultimate change … we are called to transfiguration even though we seem an eternity from its accomplishment.'[2]

The poet George Herbert wrote, 'Teach me my God and king in *all* things thee to see.' From the perspective of that mountain top there are not two worlds – sacred and secular – for since in Christ God has entered our world, it is not for us to call anything 'profane that God has touched' (Acts 10:15). Isaiah, in his temple vision, learned that quite literally 'the *whole* earth is full of his glory' (Isaiah 6:3). There really is glory under our feet at every step on the road, for those with eyes to see it.

As we begin to see material things, life, money, sex and so forth from this perspective we move from mere indifferent observation to wonder, worship and adoration. None of these things are ours by right: they are gifts to be received with thankfulness and gladness of heart. A thankful heart brings a blessing to every gift. Such an outlook brings a radically new attitude to the whole of life. We move from grudging, grumbling and grabbing to gratitude; from possessiveness to praise and thankfulness. If we continue down that road we shall soon end up handling every aspect of life very differently, thinking not about what I can get, but rather about what I can give. As Jesus told us, 'Freely have you received, freely give' (Matthew 10:8).

That whole new outlook on the whole of life which comes from vision and wonder and worship is called in Greek *metanoia*. This word is generally translated as 'repentance', but really it means 'a change of outlook' resulting from a new insight. Only such a new vision of God's world will bring about a new outlook – a true transformation of society.

When the Church is transfigured through the vision of prayer and worship, society may begin to see in Christians a totally different way of life, which in turn could lead the world to stop and think it out all over again – to have second thoughts, as we say, to move from *paranoia* to *metanoia*.

Renewal

'Why was I created?' asks the Scottish Catechism. The answer is, 'I was created in order to worship God and to *enjoy* him for ever.' Or, as the psychiatrist in Peter Shaffer's play, *Equus*, comments: 'If you don't worship, you'll shrink – it's as brutal as that!' All human beings were created for worship, ecstasy and self-transcendence. However, if we do not worship the true and living God, it does not follow that we shall not worship at all. Rather, we shall worship false gods – substitutes, things which give us a fix – such as alcohol, drugs, sex, money and ambition. When we worship false gods, we become in bondage to them, whereas when we worship the one true living God he gives us back an ever-increasing freedom to *enjoy* and delight in all the other experiences of life. Enjoyment, delight and true worship all belong together. The compulsive drinker does not *enjoy* drink!

When we worship the living God, we experience self-transcendence. We are, as Charles Wesley said, 'lost in wonder, love and praise'. In a word, we are ecstatic. And as Jesus reminds us, it is only in losing our old selves that we discover and find our new and true selves. When God's people come fully alive in worship they become the sort of people that God created them to be.

Healing

Bishop John V. Taylor believes that 'there is nothing more needed by humanity today … than the recovery of a sense of "beyond-ness" in the whole of life to revive the springs of wonder and adoration.'[3] True worship is holistic – the whole person is involved in it as we love God with our whole heart and mind and with all our passions, and as we love our neighbours as ourselves.

Transcendent worship involves both heart and mind. It releases us from the tyranny of the cerebral and opens up a full self-expression as the whole body – both personal and corporate – is caught up in the transcendent. The inhibitions and barriers on that long road from head to heart are broken down – often with tears, tongues, laughter or singing. There is something very healing and wholesome about the transcendent worship and love of God for his own sake.

Evangelism

The face and image of a praying Church will be changed into the likeness of the face of the God whom we are worshipping, and the outside world will begin to make again the connection between the face and image of Christ and the face and image of his Church. It is that credibility gap between the face of Jesus and the perceived image of his Church which is the greatest single obstacle to faith and evangelization. 'Sirs, we would see Jesus' has always been the cry of all enquirers into the Christian faith, and where else can such enquirers turn, except to the Church which is called 'the Body of Christ' and which should rightly be recognized as such?

Questions for Personal Reflection or Discussion in Groups

1. In what sense would you say that many of the problems facing society today are not simply economic, but rather spiritual at root?

2. If you accept the thesis that worship is fundamental to the human condition, what place should it have in the national curriculum of our schools?

3. What is likely to happen if the instinct for worship is frustrated or not given appropriate expression? If ecstasy (not the drug variety) and self-transcendence are fundamental to health and a full human life, where are people likely to go to find it, if they are not finding it in and through the worship of the Church?

CHAPTER 2

From Longing to Belonging

And as the men were parting from him, Peter said to Jesus, 'Master, it is well that we are here; let us make three booths, one for you and one for Moses and one for Elijah' – not knowing what he said.

(LUKE 9:33)

All our longing is a longing to belong. 'It is not good for man to be alone,' said the Lord God in his concern for Adam (Genesis 2:18). In the intimacy of the original Garden of Eden there was a strong sense of communion and community between God and all his creatures. However, through Adam's sin both community and communion were fragmented, and mankind now instead experienced isolation and alienation. Competitive individualism was born!

Human beings were now cut off from one another and from God, but we have never lost that original longing to belong. There is a hole in the heart of all of us which will never be satisfied with anything less than what we were made to be – namely, persons in relationship, in communion and community. We only become truly who we are when we are in relationship with others. 'Tell me your friends, and I'll tell you what you are,' we rightly say.

God the Blessed Trinity has revealed himself as persons in relationship – love given and received in the embrace of the greater love. At the heart of the universe love is given and received within love, without loss, weariness or death. God's love was revealed to Moses as a burning bush, burning but not burnt out – the very opposite, in fact, of our human experience, in which we often end up being burnt out by our relationships with one another.

Little wonder, therefore, that when the three disciples experienced that kind of homecoming with Jesus on the mountain top, in fellowship and communion with Moses and Elijah, they experienced a kind of homesickness for heaven and felt that at last they had found where they belonged. Naturally, Peter did not want this experience to end. He had come home at last and had found his true place in the very heart of God himself, which is where, in the end, we all belong. All our longing faces in two directions. It remembers in some strange and distant way that sense of belonging which once upon a time we all knew with Adam and Eve, but it also longs and yearns for that ultimate sense of belonging within God and in heaven at the end of time.

The so-called 'rich young ruler' in the gospels was really nothing of the sort. In fact, he was just a poor, sad old thing! The epitaph on his tomb might well have been: 'He longed to belong: he ended up belonging to his belongings.' In his work *The Fire of Love* the fourteenth-century mystic Richard Rolle summarized the human dilemma in a way which speaks directly to our own age: 'Since the human soul is capable of receiving God alone, nothing less than God can fill it; which explains why lovers of earthly things are never satisfied.'

Jesus promises us that 'In my Father's house are many resting places' (John 14:2) or 'caravan sites' or 'motels' where we can put up for a night to recover our energies for the journey on the road which lies ahead. Transfiguration is a recurring experience on that road; it affords opportunities for renewal, refreshment, encouragement and re-envisioning. But we must not get into the real-estate business and seek to build permanent residences. We are a pilgrim people, with our tents and tent-pegs! The true Church must always be a Church on the move, learning to live with provisionality. Our permanent resting place, where all our longing to belong will be fulfilled, will be in the heavenly Jerusalem – the Jerusalem above, which is the mother of all our longings and strivings (see Galatians 4:25).

Renewal

God has revealed himself as 'persons in community'. We are made in his image, and so we can only become fully human by being in relationship with others, in communion and community with our fellow humans as well as with God. It follows, therefore, that the regeneration of our community life, both in the cities and in the rural areas, lies at the heart of the well-being of our society and our world. Competitive independence will bring sickness and weariness to our society, while inter-dependent complementarity will bring a new fullness of life and a richer cultural environment. We must resist the idea that communities should be sacrificed on the altar of economic expediency, or any other kind of expediency. The renewal and regeneration of our community life will need to be at the top of the agenda as we reshape and refashion our cities, our rural areas and our corporate life – economically and socially. Our concern for the homeless should not simply be sentimental, but theological. In the musical version of Dickens' *Oliver Twist* the character Oliver experiences good news when he is offered a home and a family – albeit a corrupt one: 'Consider yourself at home' the song goes; 'consider yourself part of the furniture; we've taken to you so strong; it's clear we're going to get along.'

Healing

Sin brings alienation and division and debilitates our human resources as we disperse our energies in seeking to do our own thing. The human race comes into its own when it is essentially personal and corporate at the same time – which, incidentally, is the very opposite of being individualistic or collective. When any one part of the Body – whether the physical, political or mystical – begins to play the tyrant over the rest of the members, then sickness is never far away. We are out of joint and dis-eased. Reconciliation brings healing and a fullness of life expressed through new energies and exciting enterprises.

In that corporate enterprise we discover, in fact, that the rich need the poor at least as much as the poor need the rich; that the young need the old as much as the old need the young; that the strong need the weak as much as the weak need the strong. This interplay of interdependence is the heartbeat of community life. It brings out the best in people, because they know that they belong to the larger picture and have a unique and particular role to play within the greater whole. Individualism is less than life as God intends us to live it.

Evangelism

Perhaps the only way to commend the gospel and the good news of God's Kingdom is for every congregation and community of faith to be a place where outsiders can belong. 'The only hermeneutic of the gospel,' wrote Lesslie Newbigin, 'is a congregation of men and women who believe it and live by it.'[1] Of course, preaching and proclamation are central to evangelization, yet effective evangelization will always be the life-style of the local community of faith before it is the rhetoric of the itinerant evangelist.

The local congregation of men and women living the life-style of the coming Kingdom of God – that 'end in the middle' again – will be a far better advertisement for the gospel than any amount of talk about God. There is a hole in the heart of all people, and only belonging to a community which loves and cares can begin to fill that hole and so sustain pilgrims for that greater journey to their true home in heaven.

Questions for Personal Reflection or Discussion in Groups

1. How can you have an identity if you do not know where you belong and where you are really at home? What are the reasons which should compel us to fight homelessness?

2. What do you think are the factors which are destroying community life in our nation today – both in the inner cities and in the rural areas?

3. What is the good news for single people, widows, single-parent families and other groups of people who tend to be marginalized?

4. Can you describe the good features of the gang mentality and the ghetto mentality as well as their destructive and bad features?

5. Reflect upon how a spiritually bankrupt society will inevitably become greedy, acquisitive and materialistic. What steps can we take to address this situation?

CHAPTER 3

From Learning to Knowledge

*As he [Peter] said this, a cloud came and overshadowed
them; and they were afraid as they entered the cloud.*

(LUKE 9:34)

Learning about Jesus and knowing Jesus are two very
different matters. Just before the disciples arrived at
the mountain of the transfiguration, they had been
in Caesarea Philippi, where Peter had confessed that
Jesus was the Messiah. In response Jesus had disclosed that such 'knowledge' was not the ordinary
kind of knowledge about this or that, but was rather
the sort of 'inside knowledge' that could only come
as a gift from God. This kind of knowledge could not
be achieved – it could only be received.

For it is possible to know a lot of facts about someone and never really come to know them. In French,
there are two different words for these two different

kinds of knowledge: *savoir* is the collection of facts about someone or something, while *connaître* is deep, personal and intimate knowledge.

In the King James Version of the Bible, when told that she is to be pregnant, Mary asks the angel of the annunciation, 'How can this be, since I do not *know* a man?' (Luke 1:34) – this is 'to know' in the second sense, namely to have a deep personal relationship with a man, or more literally, to have sexual intercourse with a man.

The Holy Spirit who 'overshadowed' Mary at the conception of Jesus also 'overshadowed' (it is the same word in Greek) the three disciples in the cloud. They had an awesome, intimate experience of God – this was knowledge of God in the deeper sense. Not unnaturally, the disciples 'were afraid'. They understood what the psalmist had meant when he wrote, 'Such knowledge is too wonderful for me' (Psalm 139). It was all too much for them. T. S. Eliot was quite right when he said, 'Humankind cannot bear very much reality.'

As John V. Taylor shows in his book, *The Go-Between God*, this kind of inside knowledge is nothing less than a gift of the Holy Spirit, who builds relationships between people and personalizes the universe.[1] It is the Holy Spirit who makes the world come alive for us. The Holy Spirit overshadows God's people, giving them the precious gift of wisdom – something far greater than mere knowledge and far deeper than simply the facts of the matter.

Our yearning for God will never be satisfied solely by intellectual and cerebral searchings. Augustine said, 'Our hearts are restless till they rest in God,' and that has indeed been the experience of countless millions of men and women throughout the ages. We naturally yearn for that deep, inner and personal knowledge of God. God says, 'Be still and *know* [in this second sense] that I am God' (Psalm 46:10). There are some things which can only be communicated 'face to face', as we say. This is a form of communication which is only possible in deep communion with another. Frequently it is beyond words and takes place in silence.

Peter, reflecting on the Transfiguration experience many years later, said: 'We did not follow cleverly devised myths, when we made known to you the power and coming of our Lord Jesus Christ, but we were eye-witnesses of his majesty' (2 Peter 1:16).

Healing

There is much talk today about the two sides of the brain – the left-hand side and the right-hand side. The left-hand side motivates the right hand and the didactic, practical, prosaic, factual and verbal side of our lives. The right-hand side motivates the left hand and the poetic, intuitive side of our lives. Factual knowledge is dealt with by one side of us, while intimate, intuitive, inside knowledge is dealt with by the other side of us. There are two sides to all of us, as we say!

Since the Age of Reason, in the Western world, education has tended to focus more upon one side than the other, being concerned primarily with the facts and with building up knowledge about various subjects – especially scientific subjects – while we have played down worship, prayer and the poetic and intuitive side of human nature. Not surprisingly, this has crippled us and lamed us. Health and healing come through an holistic approach to life, from a proper balance between both sides of our nature. The paralysis of unending analysis inhibits growth, with its accompanying capacity for worship, love and adoration.

In the past people used to talk about the head and the heart, rather than the two sides of the human brain, but it amounts to the same thing. So Bishop Theophan tells us that when we pray we should stand 'before God with our head in our heart'. And this should be so not only when we pray. We need to be 'centred' much more in our everyday life rather than 'strung out' – as we often say and often are.

It is important each day to find a quiet time and a quiet space in which to wait upon God, and to be still in his presence. Many Christians use the Jesus Prayer (a simple prayer from the Eastern Church: 'Lord Jesus Christ, Son of the Living God, have mercy on me, a sinner'), or a mantra (a word or a short phrase which is repeated many times), or the rosary, or they simply repeat the name 'Jesus'. This gives the left side of the brain something to get on with quite me-chanically, while the intuitive and worship side of the mind quietly opens (like a flower in the sunshine) in the presence of God, engaging in wordless worship, wonder, love and praise.

'To sing is to pray twice,' said St Augustine. Today he might well have said, 'To sing is to pray with both sides of the brain.' For music has a capacity for bringing about a healing self-transcendence, which is why its place in formal worship is so very important. The secular world has discovered in recent years that music can help to heal the lopsided casualties of our age, bringing a measure of reconciliation between the conflicting sides of our nature.

Renewal

Throughout the history of the Christian Church, whenever renewal and revival have been happening, they have always been expressed through music in worship. Whether we look to the Gregorian chant of the sixth century or to the charismatic songs of the twentieth century or to any other age, the evidence is the same: when we sing, we are released into deeper worship from the heart.

All this new emphasis upon worship as the way to a knowledge and experience of God has been focused in the remarkable phenomenon of the Protestant community at Taizé, in France. Since the end of the Second World War, when the community was founded, it has attracted many thousands of young people. Through its monastic worship – with both its music and its silence – Taizé has given them an inner experience of God. Until the Church is transfigured in and through its worship it will have nothing of any distinctive significance to offer the world at large.

Evangelism

The saying goes, 'Don't preach about Christianity: preach Christ.' For it is possible to teach all kinds of interesting and confusing doctrines – 'cleverly devised myths' – all in the name of Christianity and to engage in great learned debates about it, without ever having experienced a personal encounter with Christ – without ever coming 'to know him more clearly, love him more dearly and follow him more nearly.'

Evangelism is making Christ himself known, not simply divulging facts about him. His promise is still true: 'I, if I be lifted up, will draw all men and women to myself' (John 12:32). Paul says factual knowledge, by itself, simply puffs one up (1 Corinthians 8:1). So the theologian is someone who knows God. As Evagrius of Pontus said, 'If you pray truly you are a theologian.' Right prayer brings true knowledge of God.

We shall commend the gospel of Jesus Christ to this generation perhaps more through the door of one side of the brain than through the other, which has hitherto tended to be our exclusive emphasis. There is always a place for conveying the truth through words – through personal witness or through preaching. That will speak to some people, sometimes. And yet, in this modern age we shall commend the gospel at least as much, if not more, by saying in effect, 'Come and see' – by inviting people with possibly little or no experience of worship to engage in worship with the heart as well as the head, through silence as well as song, and through wordless attention to enter fully into communion with the living God.

Questions for Personal Reflection or Discussion in Groups

1. What do you think are the most important ingredients for a balanced education?
2. Do you think the over-emphasis on technology is damaging interpersonal relationships? How is it affecting community life, both locally and nationally?

3. If your experience of prayer and worship has been very rational or 'left-brain', why not try experimenting with more 'right-brain' approaches to prayer? For example, create a small 'prayer corner' in your home, with an icon, a candle, an open Bible and flowers, as a focus for prayer at all times. Try making more use of songs, poetry and repetitive prayers, such as the 'Jesus prayer'.

CHAPTER 4

From Listening to Obeying

And a voice came out of the cloud, saying, 'This is my Son, my Chosen; listen to him!'

(LUKE 9:35)

The twentieth century is an age of information. Through TV advertisements, fax machines, telephones, E-mail and the Internet we are being continuously bombarded with data. Yet information is not the same as revelation. God is not interested in giving us endless information about himself – which we can then choose to ignore, for all practical purposes.

'But be doers of the word and not hearers only,' says St James in his epistle (James 1:22). Mary the mother of Jesus was a doer of the word. She took God at his word when she said, 'Be it unto me according to thy word' (Luke 1:38). She was obedient to that word and so could speak with great authority to the servants at the wedding feast when she said, pointing to Jesus, the Word of God, 'Do whatever he tells you' (John 2:5).

Jesus is God's last word to us – a word of good news. The words of the Father spoken at Christ's baptism and at his transfiguration are words of loving reassurance. God's word to Jesus and to the whole human race (whether Christian, or of another religion, or of none) is just quite simply: 'I love you.' 'In this is love,' says John in his first epistle, 'not that we loved God, but that he loved us' (1 John 4:10). That is the only sure foundation on which we can build our lives – the assurance that we are loved infinitely by the One who knows all.

In our baptism, as on Calvary Hill, God declares his infinite love for us and his readiness to forgive all our sins once and for all. Our obedience is not, therefore, the result of the rules and regulations of a religion, but rather the result of a loving relationship of faith and trust in the One who has declared his love for us. 'The love of Christ constrains us,' says St Paul (2 Corinthians 5:14).

Yet obedience and authority are interwoven. Mary speaks with authority to those servants because she speaks as one who is herself under authority. Jesus, especially in the Fourth Gospel, is clearly seen as having put himself voluntarily under the authority of the Father, and so he speaks nothing of himself (John 7:16f.). The Church has no authority of its own with which to speak; its only authority is that which God gives to it and which it receives through loving obedience.

For authority is what happens to power when it is freely given away. God in Christ has emptied himself of his power and has become like one of the powerless (Philippians 2:7). It is through that conversion of power that Jesus speaks with an ageless authority, to which men and women have not only listened, but to which they have also willingly and gladly given their unqualified obedience.

The Church has been most corrupt in those chapters in its history when it has grasped at and wielded worldly power. Only an obedient Church will speak with authority to the world about the things of God. We listen to Jesus, the Word made flesh, *through* the words of Scripture, and we ask for God's grace and strength to reorder and refashion our lives to bring them into line with that same living Word, which, like Mary, we ponder in our hearts (Luke 2:51) and also show forth in our daily lives.

Renewal

Paul wrote, 'All scripture is inspired by God and profitable for teaching, for reproof, for correction, and for training in righteousness' (2 Timothy 3:16). The Scriptures are a book of presence, and throughout history, whenever and wherever the people of God have opened the Scriptures and read them under the Spirit of God, God's Word – Jesus – has made himself known and present. So we should speak of the real presence of Jesus *through* Scripture, in a way very similar to the way in which we rightly speak of the real presence of Jesus *through* the sacraments.

So properly regarded, the Scriptures, like the sacraments, constitute an icon. You are not supposed to look *at* an icon but *through* it, as if it were a window otherwise we turn an icon into an idol. So Jesus himself warns us against searching *in* the Scriptures for eternal life: 'You search the scriptures, because you think that *in* them you have eternal life; and it is they that bear witness to me; yet you refuse to come to me that you may have eternal life' (John 5:39).

Both personal renewal in Christian discipleship as well as corporate renewal for the whole Church come about whenever we take God at his Word and so begin to be 'doers of the word and not hearers only'.

Healing

When God's Word is spoken with authority, it is an effective Word which achieves what it commands. From the outset, in the book of Genesis, we see the power of God's Word to accomplish his command: 'God said, "Let there be light", and there was light.'

So in chapter 2 of Mark's Gospel, Jesus displays the power and authority of his word in front of the Pharisees when he says:

'Which is easier, to say to the paralytic, "Your sins are forgiven" or to say, "Rise, take up your pallet and walk"? But that you may know that the Son of Man has authority on earth to forgive sins …' Then he said to the paralytic, 'I say to you, rise, take up your pallet and go home.' And he rose.

(MARK 2:9–12)

God has given to his Church that same authority to forgive sins and to heal. Often the two are interconnected. All sin brings dis-ease, though we must not reverse the argument and claim that all disease is the direct result of the patient's sin. 'All authority has been given to me,' claims the ascending Christ (Matthew 28:18). On a previous occasion he gives that authority to his wondering apostles: 'Receive the Holy Spirit. If you forgive the sins of any, they are forgiven; if you retain the sins of any, they are retained' (John 20:23).

In so far, then, as forgiveness and healing are inter-related, the Church has been commissioned with a ministry of healing, through its ordained ministry as well as through the charismatic ministry of healing which is given to many men and women as a special gift to be exercised with generosity and humility.

It is perhaps significant that we find in the Epistle of St James the mandate for the practice of the very early Church with regard to the healing ministry: 'Is any among you sick? Let him call for the elders of the church, and let them pray over him, anointing him with oil in the name of the Lord' (James 5:14).

Evangelism

The old familiar hymn says, 'Tell me the old, old story of Jesus and his love.' The Scriptures are the record, largely in story form, of God's dealings with his people throughout the centuries. The Scriptures only make full sense to us when we see them in relation to the once-for-all story of Jesus and his resurrection (see Luke 24:27). Yet there is a third story – our personal story, the story of God's dealings with each and every one of us. In many ways our personal stories have a similar outline and profile to both the story of God's people throughout the ages and the particular story of Jesus 'and his love'.

Laurens Van der Post has remarked, 'If you've not got a story to tell, you've not got a life to live.' Whenever God's people come together to worship and to celebrate, they delight to tell their story from the Scriptures. As we remember that story we recover our identity as God's chosen people – chosen for service and not for privilege. The liturgy selects many passages of Scripture for reading aloud and singing about. Together we remember *our* resurrection story as God's chosen people, beginning in

Genesis and Israel's history and culminating in the story of Jesus' life, death and resurrection.

Jesus himself did not write a book. Instead he formed a community – a community of the resurrection – which in turn was formed and fashioned by God's Word, revealed through the words of Scripture. Only a scriptural Church will be an evangelistic Church.

Questions for Personal Reflection or Discussion in Groups

1. What would you say are the important features in the story of the healing of the centurion's servant in Matthew 8:5–13?

2. Can you suggest different ways of reading and learning Scripture? What do you know of the Eastern Church's way of using icons in worship?

3. Take a look at James 5:16. In what practical ways can the Church recover its former emphasis upon the centrality of the healing ministry? Do you think there is a connection between reconciliation and healing, and if so, what is it?

CHAPTER 5

From Loving to Commitment

And when the voice had spoken, Jesus was found alone.

(LUKE 9:36)

'You are my beloved, my chosen,' are the words of the Father. Immediately after those words of reassurance had been spoken, Moses and Elijah faded into the background and the disciples saw only Jesus. The coming of Jesus marks the end of all religions and philosophies: the law and the prophets (Moses and Elijah) find their fulfilment in the revelation of the glory of God in the face of Jesus.

We sometimes say to the parent of a child, 'He or she has eyes only for you.' Indeed, when we are truly in love, it is very apparent to all our friends that we have eyes only for the beloved. That is the attitude we need to have towards Jesus: we must have eyes only for him.

In English we talk about *falling* in love; many other languages have expressions about love which include this idea of falling over. Sometimes God's love for us will affect us physically. One of the famous icons of the transfiguration shows the disciples being 'bowled over', toppling backwards down the mountainside with the impact of such love. (John, in chapter 18 of his Gospel, indicates a similar impact upon the soldiers who came to arrest Jesus in the Garden of Gethsemane. He tells us that they 'drew back and fell to the ground' when Jesus disclosed himself to them.)

There is a sense in which at some point in our Christian discipleship, we need actually to *fall in love with God*. When this happens, it generally shows itself in some physical manifestation of the body. Sometimes people fall backwards when they are 'slain in the Spirit'. Sometimes people who are being touched by God will experience a release of laughter or tears, or they may speak or sing in tongues. Love is generally expressed through one part of our body or another. Yet, of course, so is hysteria!

How are we to know the genuine from the fake in all this loving business? Real love expresses itself in total commitment. The words of the marriage vow, 'For richer, for poorer, in sickness and in health', express the essential characteristics of a Christian's love for another, reflecting the sort of constant, unconditional love which God has for us. Costly commitment, not just cautious contract, is at the heart of God's covenant. That's God's way of loving, and since we are made in his image, it is ultimately what all real loving should be like.

In God's covenant with Noah in the Old Testament, sealed in that rainbow-shaped promise, there is God's insistence that he is going to see all this loving business through to the bitter end and beyond – in a new covenant. Christian marriage is intended to be a similar sign of that kind of loving; as the old prayer book says, marriage signifies 'unto us the mystical union between Christ and his church'. If we love as God loves, we will refuse to use people for our own purposes, staying with them while the going is good, but backing out when the going gets tough.

On top of that mountain, Jesus showed his disciples a new way of loving, but he would also have pointed to that other way – the long road below the mountain leading up to Jerusalem, to conflict, failure, darkness and despair. That was the road he had to take. The way to a new and fuller life in Christ passes *right through* the dark side of life. So often, when people are going through a time of suffering, others somewhat cruelly retort, 'Oh, he or she will get over it', implying that there is a way round all this. But that is not Christ's way – his royal highway passes right through it to the light and peace beyond the conflict.

God does not send suffering or cause it. Rather, he shows us what he can do with it for us, if we stay committed to him, in the same way as he has committed himself to us. For in the end the crucifixion was not a Bad Friday but a Good Friday, when seen in the light of everything which happened afterwards – the resurrection, the ascension and the glorification of our humanity back home in the heart of God. From the perspective of the resurrection, with hindsight, we can see that '*all* things work together for good' (Romans 8:28). That is what transfiguration is all about: seeing everything (warts and all) in the light of the resurrection. So the light on the mountain top streamed back into history from beyond the cross – the 'end in the middle' – turning all the sadness and dereliction into glory.

It is the light shining through the broken pieces of glass which constitutes the magic and beauty of the kaleidoscope. The broken pieces of our humanity are precious to God, and his work is to gather up the fragments that remain so that in the end nothing is lost (John 6:12). That process requires a deep-down loving, expressed through unconditional commitment and covenanted love.

As the hymn says, 'O love that will not let me go, I hang my weary soul on thee. I trace the rainbow through the rain, and feel the promise is not vain that morn shall tearless be.' Transfiguration is the light of the resurrection shining through the tears of God *in* the pain of the world, showing a rainbow of new hope and confidence in the outcome of all history.

Renewal

Renewal is not the same as revival. Revival merely means coming back to life. Jesus did not die and come back to life – there would have been no good news in that. Lazarus came back to life. But Jesus died and was raised to *new life* on the other side of death – to that fuller, richer and more abundant life which we call eternal life. It is a new *quality* of life, not just a greater *quantity* of life.

Neither revival nor mere survival constitute good news. Immortality, if it means just going on going on, would not be good news either. I need to change and be changed, and that always involves a kind of death which is much more than just the grave. Renewal and resurrection take us straight *through* all the darkness and the pain so that we may be raised to a new quality of life on the other side of all our deaths, including the grave. Jesus promised to be with us all *through* this.

Healing

We know from the New Testament records just about all we really need to know about this resurrection business. In John's Gospel we are told that in his resurrection appearances to his disciples, Jesus showed them the wounds which the nails of the cross had made in his body. The musical *Jesus Christ Superstar* is misnamed. Jesus is not a glamorous superstar. He still bears in his transfigured body the marks of love – the cost of loving. Yet by some strange divine chemistry those wounds, those scars, have become stars. They have been incorporated into the design of the risen body of Christ and have been transfigured quite wonderfully.

In the Christian understanding of healing there is a strong measure of homeopathic thinking – you work with the grain and not against it. Problems are often solutions in disguise, and so it is with pain: aches and pains are often blessings in disguise. Grace perfects nature, it does not annihilate it. We shall be recognizable in our resurrection bodies; the old person will not be blotted out. Rather, we shall be transfigured. So, when Paul prayed for the 'thorn in the flesh' to be taken away, God saw fit not to remove it but simply to say to Paul, 'My grace is sufficient for you.'

Evangelism

The gospel is not so much some*thing* to swallow; it is some*one* to follow. Christianity is not an ideology, a philosophy or even a religion in the usual sense of that word. Christianity is not a *thing*: really it is a *person*: it is all about Jesus and his resurrection.

We must not allow the institutional Church to get in the way of the centrality of Jesus: 'churchianity' is no substitute for Christianity. The evangelist as well as the evangelistic church must be certain that it is Jesus we are holding up to the world and not simply doctrines – however orthodox they may be. The gospel becomes magnetic and attractive when it focuses upon the person of Jesus. All the rest, as St Paul says at the end of his ministry, is 'so much garbage compared with the knowledge of Christ' (Philippians 3:8). Paul had learned that lesson back in the days of his preaching at Corinth, where he resolved to confess only Christ and him crucified (1 Corinthians 2:2). As Cowper wrote:

The dearest idol I have known
Whate'er that idol be;
O help me tear it from thy throne
And worship only thee.

Questions for Personal Reflection
or Discussion in Groups

1. We have been created to love people and to use things. Have we ended up loving things and abusing people?

2. How can the Church demonstrate and proclaim a love which is costly and sacrificial? How can we, the Church, help to recover the Christian understanding of the sacrament of marriage? What is the place of friendship both inside and outside of marriage?

3. When means become ends, icons degenerate into idols. In what ways do you think both the Church and the world have fallen into the trap of making the means into the ends?

CHAPTER 6

From Leaving to Discipleship

*On the next day, when they had come down from the
mountain, a great crowd met Jesus.*

(LUKE 9:37)

'Tis good Lord to be here,
Though we may not remain.
Yet since thou bidst us leave the mount
Come with us to the plain.

The Jesus who had led those three disciples up
the mountain was the same Jesus who now led
them down the other side and back to the plain
below, into the crowds and all the pains and problems of everyday life. On another mountain in
Galilee – the mountain of the ascension – the same
Jesus, at the end of his earthly ministry, would
promise that he would be with his disciples to the
end of time (Matthew 28:20).

Saying goodbye is quite a heart-rending business, and not least if we have been surrounded by love, hospitality and warmth. Yet we can never be disciples of Jesus unless we are ready to let go, leave home and family and follow Jesus on the road that leads to our true home in heaven (Mark 10:29).

For Christians believe that it was for love's sake that God the Son went out of his way and left his home and his Father in the first place: 'He came down to earth from heaven, who is God and Lord of all.' 'For God so loved the world' – his created order – 'that he sent his Son into the world, not to condemn the world, but that the world through him might be saved' (John 3:16). The mission of the Church originates in the very heart of God himself, who is willing to go out of his way – all the way – for the sake of a broken and painful world.

That's not such a bad definition of mission: a love which is ready to go out of its way – to put itself out, as we say – and to leave the comfort and warmth of home and family for the sake of the larger vision. For a little while it had been heaven on earth on top of that mountain. Now it was a matter of coming down to earth with a bump.

God had been with his disciples on the mountain – there they saw something of his features and face. It was a never-to-be-forgotten eye-opener. But now and until the end of time, Jesus, who is Emmanuel or God With Us, is with us on the plain, in the crowd, amidst the pain of the world.

Jesus did not promise to give us all the answers to the world's problems. He promised something much better: he promised to be with us in the problems, to work with us to bring about the answers. Jesus is God *in* our midst; God *in* the mess which we have made of the world; God *in* the mystery. What more can we want?

On the mountain top the three disciples had been initiated into the school of contemplatives – men and women who have learned to see through every-thing, and, unlike cynics, who see nothing on the other side but darkness and despair, they had seen the glory of God in the face of Jesus on the other side of it all – for there really is another side to everything, if only we have eyes to see it. As George Herbert wrote:

A man that looks on glass
On it may stay his eye
Or if he pleaseth through it pass
And then the heaven espy.

The best missionaries are always first and foremost contemplatives. Just like those three disciples who came down from the mountain to the everyday world, we are meant to be 'God's spies' (to use Shakespeare's phrase) – men and women doing an undercover job for God! Yet unless we have learned on the mountain top how to see through everything as true contemplatives, when we come down to earth we shall fail to recognize this same Jesus in the crowd. We shall say, like those phoney religious people in Jesus' parable, 'But Lord, when did we see *thee* in prison, naked, in hospital or hungry?' And the Lord's reply is always the same: 'In so much as you did or did not do it to the least of one of these, my brothers and sisters, you did not do it to me' (see Matthew 25:31–46).

The task of the Church is to school millions of men and women every Sunday in worship, prayer and contemplation, so turning them into 'God's spies' who throughout the rest of the week will continue to worship and serve the Jesus of the mountain top *in* the midst of life, *in* the mess of life and *in* the mystery of it all, and so help to bring about the transformation of our society.

Renewal

It's very dangerous if too often we get to that stage where, as we say, we are 'up to our eyes in it'. Of course Christians need to be involved in the concerns of the world, with a passion and care for God's created order. Yet if we become lost in it all, then we will have nothing distinctive and different to offer to a lost world. We need to retreat frequently in order to advance; we need to rise above it all in order to see the point of it all, from the viewpoint of the One who first created it all.

At one point in the gospel narratives we read that the disciples had been out on a mission, preaching and teaching. On their return to base Jesus said to them, 'Come apart and rest a while' (Mark 6:31). The sabbath principle of resting, relaxing and standing back to enjoy and to delight in what you have created is a very godly instinct. God worked for six days and rested on the sabbath day. We are not intended to live to work, but rather to work in order to live, and to enjoy life to the full.

Some Christians try every so often to have what they call a 'retreat'. There are many retreat houses up and down the country which offer times of quiet and refreshment. Also there are the monasteries, many of which are delighted to offer hospitality to weary disciples so that they can 'come apart and rest awhile'. Whenever life has become 'one darned thing after another', the time has come to pull aside to get away from it all – but precisely in order to come back to it all with new energies and fresh vision. For the purpose of renewal is to equip us for mission.

Healing

We cannot bring healing to people from a safe distance. The Bible does not say, 'God so loved the world that he sent a fax'! God wants to continue Christ's work – healing the sick, comforting the bereaved, feeding the hungry, and doing all the other wonderful things we read about in the New

Testament. But he can only do it now *through* his apostolate – the men and women whom he sends on his errands of love and mercy. They are people whose hearts and lives God has touched. Jesus is still in touch with the needs of his world *through* the hands and feet and tongues of the members of his Body, the Church.

Evangelism

You are Christians
Then your Lord is one and the same
with Jesus on the throne of his glory
with Jesus in his blessed sacrament
with Jesus received into your hearts in communion,
with Jesus who is mystically with you as you pray
and with Jesus enshrined in the hearts and bodies
of his brothers and sisters up and down the world.

Now go out into the highways and hedges
and look for Jesus in the ragged and naked
in the oppressed and sweated
in those who have lost hope,
and in those who are struggling to make good.

Look for Jesus in them; and when you find him,
gird yourselves with his towel of fellowship,
and wash his feet in the person of his brethren.

(BISHOP WESTON OF ZANZIBAR)

The world needs from the Church an envisioned lay apostolate, men and women who, when the worship is over, are committed to beginning the service! We receive our commissioning for mission in the worship on the mountain top. The Holy Spirit overshadows God's people in their baptism and confirmation, just as he overshadowed Mary at the annunciation and the three disciples in the cloud at the transfiguration. After his baptism Jesus was driven by the Holy Spirit into mission and ministry. It is the same for all followers of Jesus: we were all baptized for mission and ministry.

Having worshipped Christ in the sacrament and in the sanctuary, we then go out to worship and serve this same Christ, finding him disguised as the poor and the needy, the homeless and the prisoners. Having discovered God in the highest place, we must then go and worship and serve him in the high street!

Questions for Personal Reflection
or Discussion in Groups

1. With Sunday now very much like any other day for many people, how can we celebrate it distinctively and in a way which will draw others to Christ?

2. How can we help Christians to see that the main focus for their apostolate is in their family, their workplace and the world?

3. Is the emphasis upon lay ministry today in danger of creating Church-centred Christians rather than Kingdom-centred human beings?

From Transfiguration to Transformation: Christianity as a New Way of Life

I came that they may have life, and have it abundantly.

(JOHN 10:10)

And we all, with unveiled face, beholding the glory of the Lord, are being changed into his likeness from one degree of glory to another; for this comes from the Lord who is the Spirit.

(2 CORINTHIANS 3:18)

The pilgrimage of Christian discipleship involves risk. Like Abraham, the very first pilgrim, we must step out into the unknown, expecting and accepting that change will happen and that we ourselves will be changed. 'We walk by faith and not by sight' (2

Corinthians 5:7). Our journey is one of prayer and inner reflection in which we move from one insight to another in the cloud of unknowing. From time to time we seem to catch glimpses of Jesus' face, and from time to time he disappears from our sight (see John 13:33). We have to learn to trust him even in the darkness and in the unknown. As Ann and Barry Ulanov write:

> *In praying we risk major changes by taking what seem endless small steps toward the end purpose of life. We move toward that glory in which all the words that glorify the Lord and sing God's praises seem understatements ... What was hidden is now shown to us; what was far below us in shrouded darkness is now right before us in the light. The way things appear to us and the way we appear to others have both been fundamentally changed ... 'Transfiguration' is the awesome word that best describes the changes.*[1]

Hopefully you will have found this book to be a work-book and not an armchair book, inviting stout walking shoes rather than cosy slippers.

A Rule of Life for a New Way of Life

All who have read or studied this book and who have undertaken this journey, literally or symbolically, personally or as part of a group (all the way or part of the way), are invited to test the truths expressed in the book by living the life – as the saying goes, 'If you live the life, you shall know the doctrine.' Only in this way can the Church become a community of the transfiguration and so help to bring about the transformation of society. We shall not be renewed personally or corporately as a Church by having the right opinion on any of the issues facing the Church or society today. God will show us the way if we are willing to walk in the way and to live in such a way that our eyes are constantly on Jesus, 'the author and perfecter of our faith'.

The Spine of Life

The human body without a spine could neither walk, run, nor dance – indeed, it would not be able to move at all. Similarly, many forms of plant life need a trellis or frame if they are to grow heavenwards rather than fall flat on their faces.

A rule of life is intended to be a framework which enables and fosters growth. The rule is not intended to degenerate into legalism or formalism – on the contrary, it permits freedom and growth while providing direction and purpose.

So the following simple rule of life is offered to all – lay people as well as clergy – who form a hidden community of the transfiguration. It needs adaptation to personal circumstances. In order to do this, it might be helpful to seek out a 'soul friend' or spiritual director or prayer companion.

Seven Simple Steps to Spiritual Renewal

Scripture

Read a portion of the Scriptures daily, either in the Daily Office of the Church, in Morning and Evening Prayer, or according to some other scheme of Bible study and reflection.

Sacraments

To attend the Eucharist on Sundays and greater feast days, and perhaps on one other day each week, in order to retain the vision of a life lived sacramentally and eucharistically – that is, with thanksgiving for all of God's gifts to us. When necessary we should also avail ourselves of the use of the sacraments of reconciliation and healing.

Prayer in the Spirit

Seek a time and a place at the beginning of every day for quiet prayer and reflection, for intercession and spiritual reading. Set aside a long weekend once a year for a spiritual retreat.

Study

Study our faith by regularly attending courses or by reading books which will increase our understanding of Christian belief, practice and experience.

Stewardship

As a thank-offering to God, give a portion of our time, money and talents to the work of the Church and to the extension of the Kingdom.

Sacrificial Service

Undertake special responsibilities in the wider community on a voluntary basis; or care for some person who is unable to care for themselves; or visit the sick and care for somebody in special need. Undertake our daily work in a spirit of vocation, dedication and service.

Sent Out for Life and Work in Society

Society and its concerns must necessarily be the concerns of the renewed Christian, who is *sent out* week by week to speak the good news, to show it and to share it.

~

Praying with the Icon
of the Transfiguration

Against the unchanging golden light of Heaven are silhouetted the holy things: the Holy One of God, His saving acts, the primal symbols of mountain and Glory. But, of course, it's all only paint and plaster and wood. Using an icon begins with an act of faith: that God will use it too; that He will use this humble object and our imaginative response to carry the charge of His Word. For an icon is a sort of text, and a sort of sacrament, and an adjunct and testimony to Scripture and Sacrament.

Scripture is often the best place to start. When using an icon which describes a scriptural event look at the text. No problem with the Transfiguration: there is an account in each of the Gospels. The first discovery is that a picture presents the event as a moment, not a story. That's a clue to the way we engage with an icon in prayer. An icon is a heavenly moment, and we take a little excursion out of time to join it. Perhaps we might begin by finding our way round the image, identifying the characters, perhaps even greeting them. We are their contemporaries in the heavenly moment. And not merely contemporaries: just as every Christian is 'in Christ' so, through Him every Christian is 'in Moses', 'in Elijah', 'in Peter, James, and John'. An icon gives our attention time to identify aspects of ourselves with these giants of faith, for if God's promises are true, we all are called to see God face to face, like Moses; to prepare His way, like Elijah; to strengthen the brethren, like Peter; to be beloved disciples, like John. So, an icon is a mirror. The gold reflects our true worth in the context of God's promise.

So far, the icon has been passive and we have been active, but prayer is often not so much doing something as stopping doing something. Here an icon can offer help by example. We look at it, and it looks at us. It is unmoving. It has all the time in the world. Perhaps it's just that an icon gives us something, not too strenuous, to do with our consciousness while God gets to work at deeper levels.

Finally, and perhaps more effectively than formal prayer and meditation, there is the use of the icon simply to register the presence of the Holy in our home. Human beings are uncomfortable with the Holy. It worries us; it reproaches us; in other cultures it terrifies us or drives us mad. God loves us, He is not proud. He wants us to be in every sense familiar with Him. He wants to be part of our family. An icon in the corner of the room means just that: the Holy as part of the family; an effectual sign of the incarnation. Of course, most of the time the Holy will be ignored. God doesn't mind that. But sometimes, when we glance at the icon we will remember Him. And sometimes we might want to say something to ourselves, or to God. Then, let the icon turn us back again to Scripture:

I am fearfully and wonderfully made.

(PSALM 139:14)

In your light we see light.

(PSALM 36:9)

Behold my servant, whom I uphold.

(ISAIAH 42:1)

We shall be like him, for we shall see him as he is.

(1 JOHN 2:3)

Dom Anselm Shobrook OSB

A Prayer with the Icon

Holy One,
In the Transfiguration of Jesus, our brother and our
Lord, we have seen God in the heart of Humanity and
Humanity in the heart of God.

By following your Child, your Son in all his humanity,
in life and through death, may we too discover and dis-
close your everlasting Glory.

We ask this in his name, who lives and reigns with you
in the unity of the Holy Spirit.

Amen.

Notes

Chapter 1: From Looking to Worshipping

1. Sermon 103.
2. *Primary Speech: A Psychology of Prayer*, London, SCM Press, 1985, p. 116.
3. *The Go-Between God*, John V. Taylor, SCM Press, 1972, p. 45.

Chapter 2: From Longing to Belonging

1. *The Gospel in a Pluralist Society*, Lesslie Newbigin, William B. Eerdmans, Grand Rapids, Michigan, 1989, p. 227.

Chapter 3: From Learning to Knowledge

1. SCM Press, 1972.

Epilogue: From Transfiguration to Transformation

1. *Primary Speech: A Psychology of Prayer*, SCM Press, London, 1985, pp. 116–17.